Start TO Finish
Second Series

Food

FROM Milk TO Ice Cream

STACY TAUS-BOLSTAD

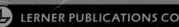 LERNER PUBLICATIONS COMPANY Minneapolis

Lerner Publications Company
A division of Lerner Publishing Group, Inc.
241 First Avenue North
Minneapolis, MN 55401 U.S.A.

Website address: www.lernerbooks.com

Photo Acknowledgments
The images in this book are used with the permission of: © iStockphoto.com/Daniel Loiselle, p. 1; © Royalty-Free/CORBIS, p. 3; © iStockphoto.com/Zmeel Photography, p. 5; © Todd Strand/Independent Picture Service, pp. 7, 9, 13, 15, 17, 21; © Trinity Muller/Independent Picture Service, pp. 11, 19; © iStockphoto.com/Rosemarie Gearhart, p. 23.

Front cover: © AGphotographer/Shutterstock.com.

Main body text set in Arta Std Book 20/26.
Typeface provided by International Typeface Corp.

Library of Congress Cataloging-in-Publication Data

Taus-Bolstad, Stacy.
    From milk to ice cream / by Stacy Taus-Bolstad.
       p. cm. — (Start to finish, second series. food)
    Includes index.
    ISBN 978-0-7613-9177-7 (lib. bdg. : alk. paper)
    1. Ice cream, ices, etc.—Juvenile literature. 2. Ice cream industry—Juvenile literature. I. Title.
    TX795.T2484 2013
    637'.4—dc23   2011036510

Manufactured in the United States of America
1 – DP – 7/15/12

TABLE OF Contents

Ice cream is yummy. How is it made?

A farmer milks cows.

Ice cream starts as milk. A farmer uses a machine to milk cows. The milk flows through tubes to a tank. The tank cools the milk. Trucks take the cold milk to an ice cream factory.

The milk becomes mix.

Factory workers put the milk into a **vat**. The vat looks like a huge cooking pot. Workers stir in sugar to make the milk sweet. Together, milk and sugar make ice cream mix.

The mix is heated.

Ice cream mix must get hot before it gets cold.
Heating the mix kills **germs**. Germs can make
people sick. A machine heats the mix to
make it safe to eat. Then the mix is cooled.

A worker adds flavors.

Pipes carry the mix to a new vat. A worker adds flavors to make the mix taste good. This worker is making pineapple ice cream.

The mix is stirred.

A blade stirs the flavors into the mix.
Chocolate turns the mix brown, like
chocolate milk. Strawberry turns it pink.

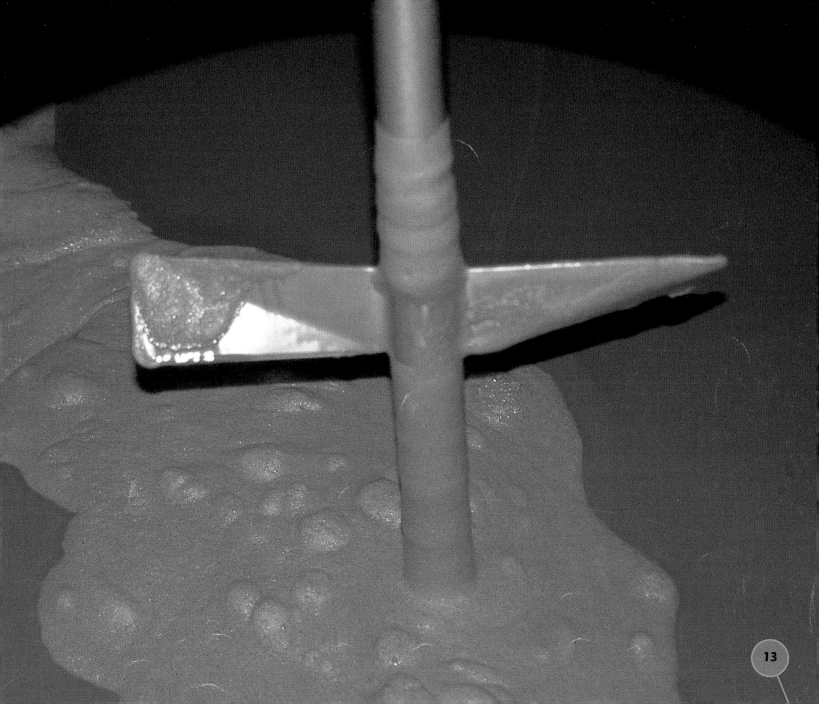

The mix gets cold.

More pipes carry the mix to a **freezer**. This machine makes the mix colder and colder. The mix turns into soft ice cream. Blades inside the freezer stir the ice cream. The blades stir in air to make the ice cream fluffy.

Ice cream fills buckets.

Empty buckets or boxes move toward another machine. The machine squirts ice cream into them. The machine in this picture can squirt chocolate and vanilla ice cream at the same time!

The ice cream gets colder.

The ice cream is still soft. It must freeze more to get harder. A worker puts the buckets into a very cold room. The room is so cold that a polar bear could live in it.

Trucks take the ice cream.

Workers load the ice cream into trucks. Each truck has a freezer to keep the ice cream cold. The trucks take the ice cream to stores.

Time for dessert!

The ice cream is ready to eat at last.
How many scoops would you like?

Glossary

flavors (FLAY-vurz): liquids added to ice cream to make it taste good

freezer (FREEZ-ur): a machine that makes food very cold

germs (JURMZ): tiny living things that can make people sick

vat (VAT): a huge pot

Index

LERNER e SOURCE

Expand learning beyond the printed book. Download free, complementary educational resources for this book from our website, www.lerneresource.com.